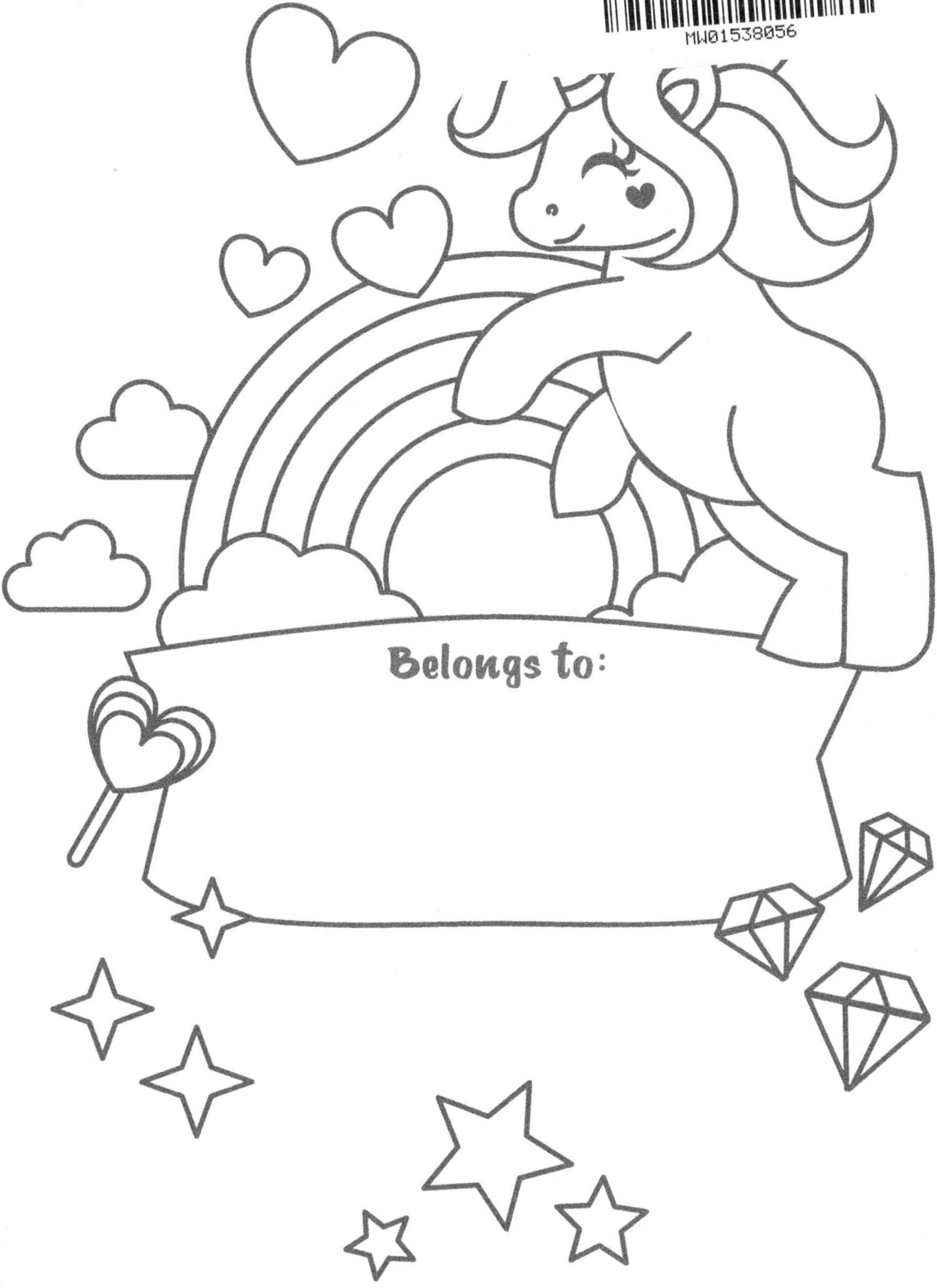
Belongs to:

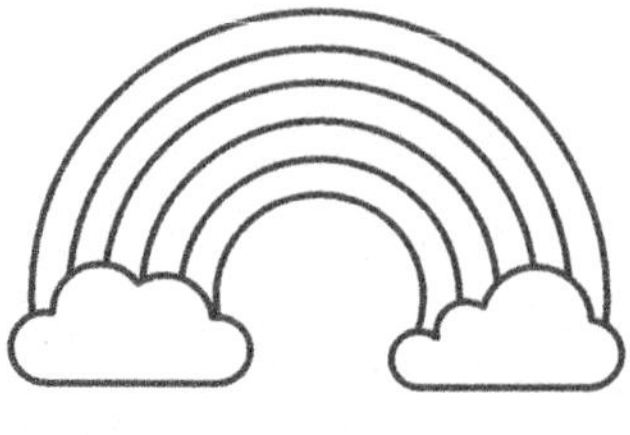

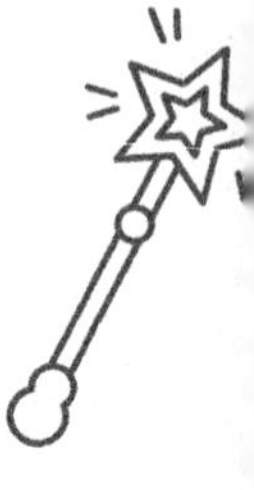

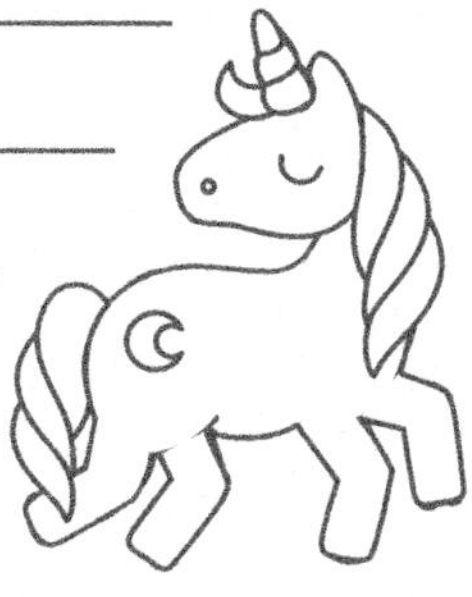

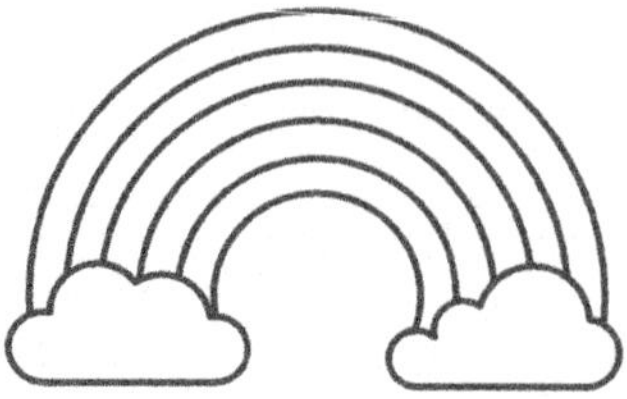

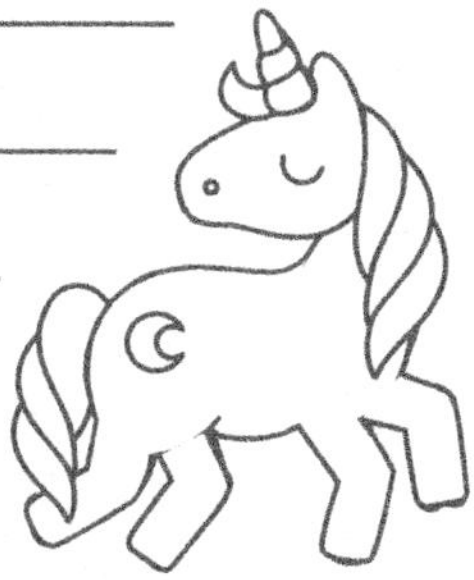

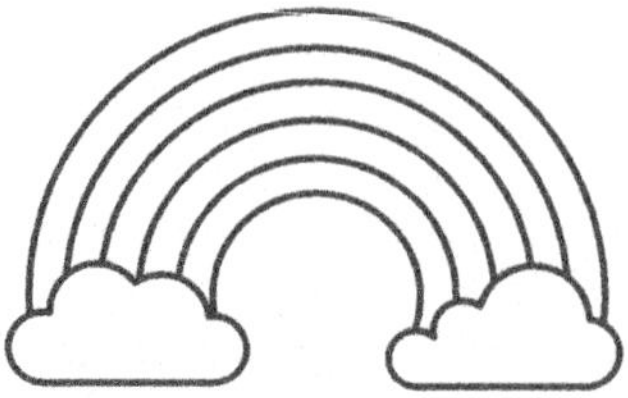
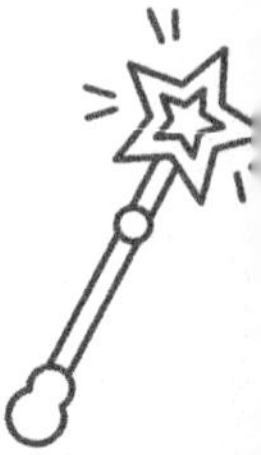

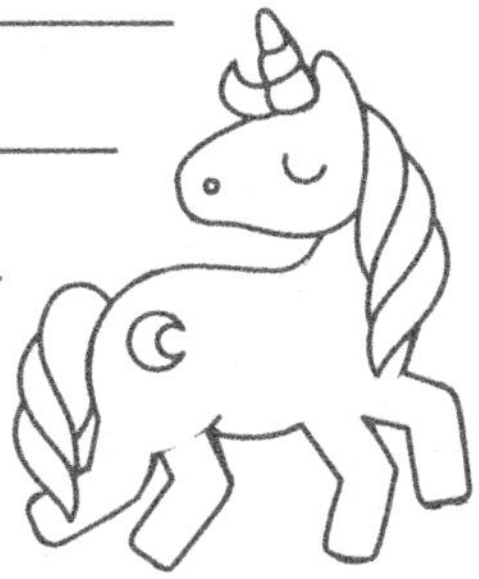

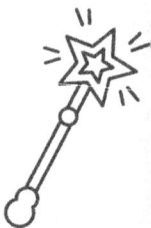

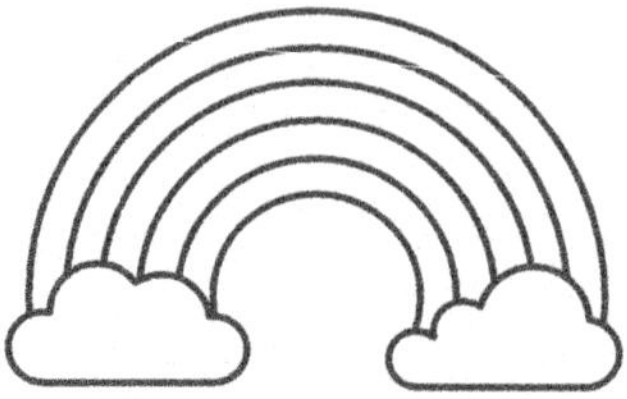

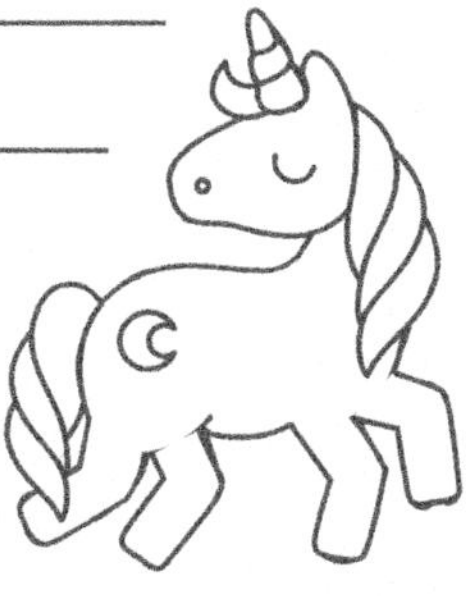

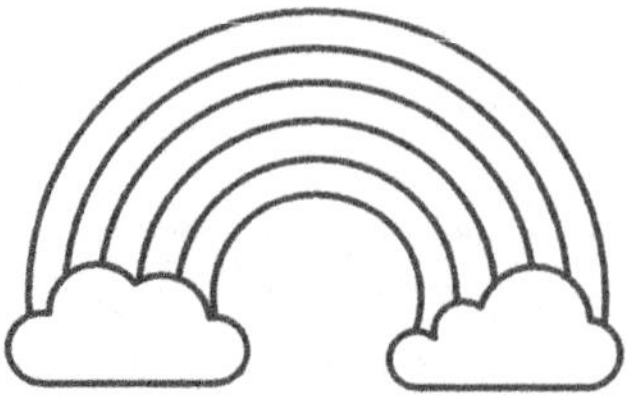

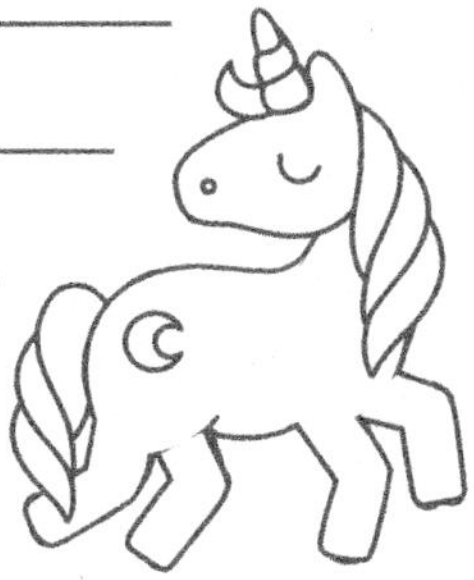

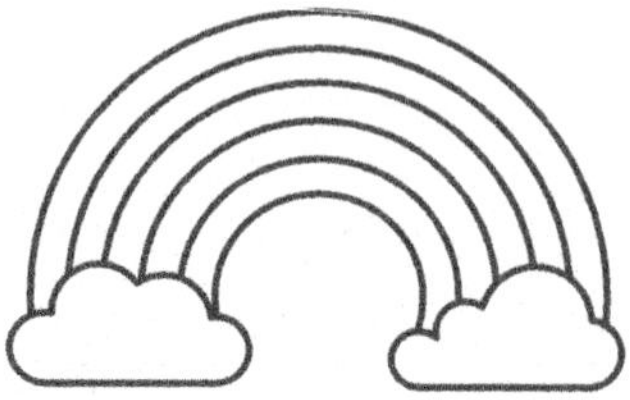
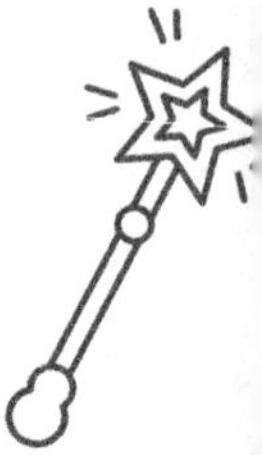

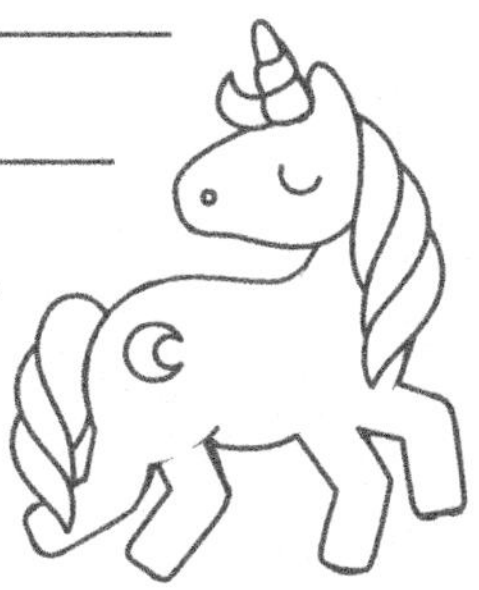

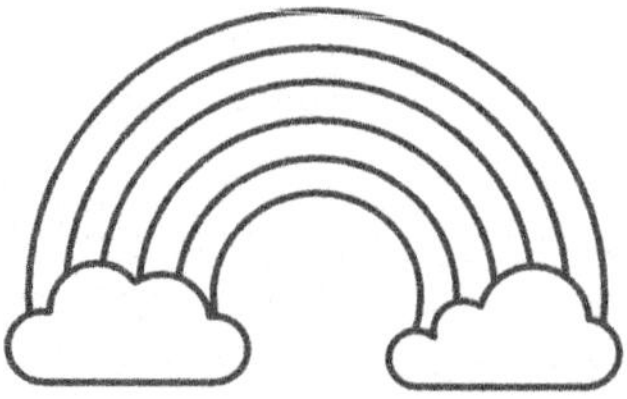

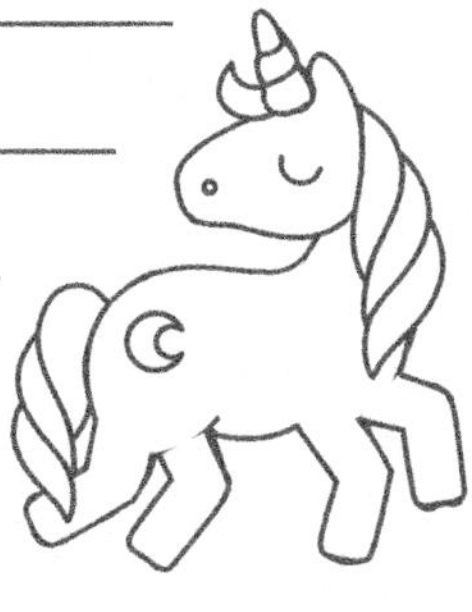

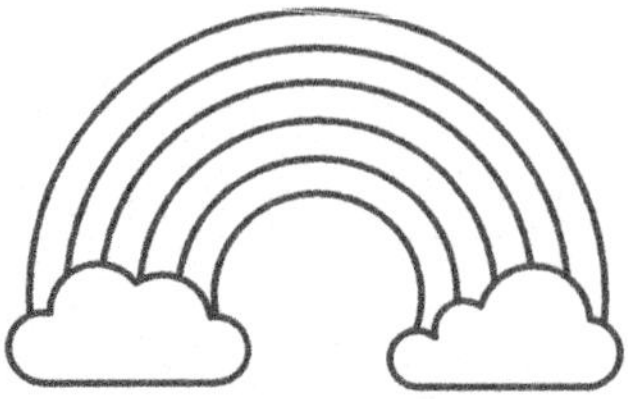

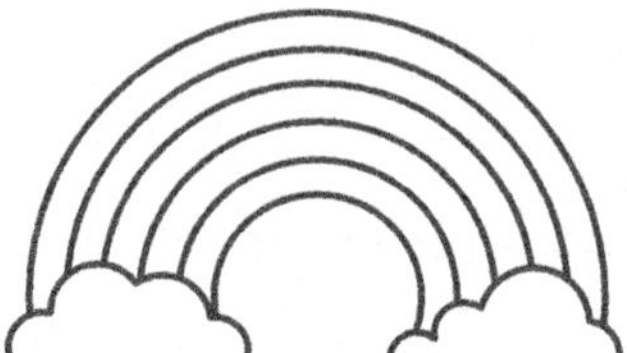

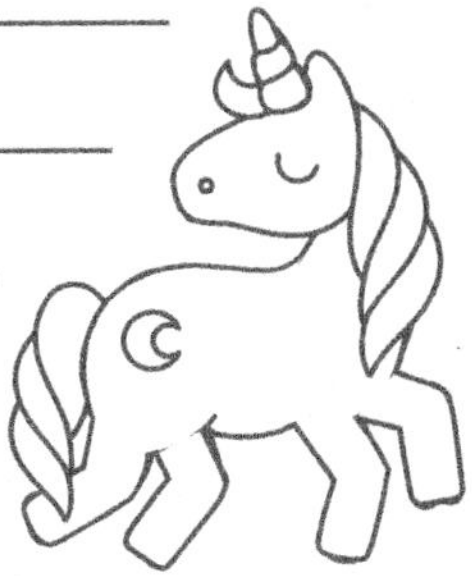

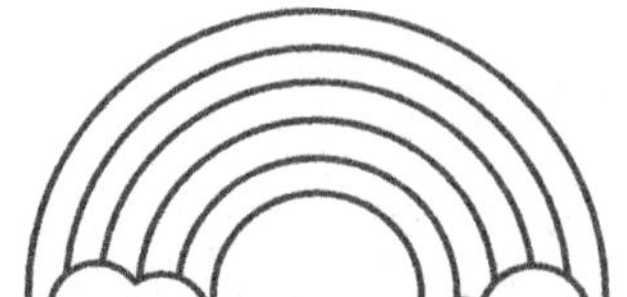

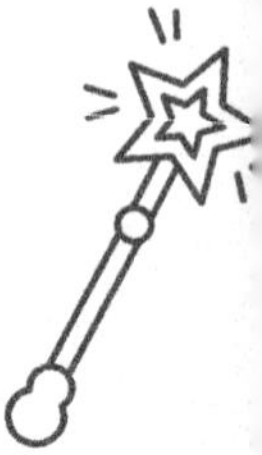

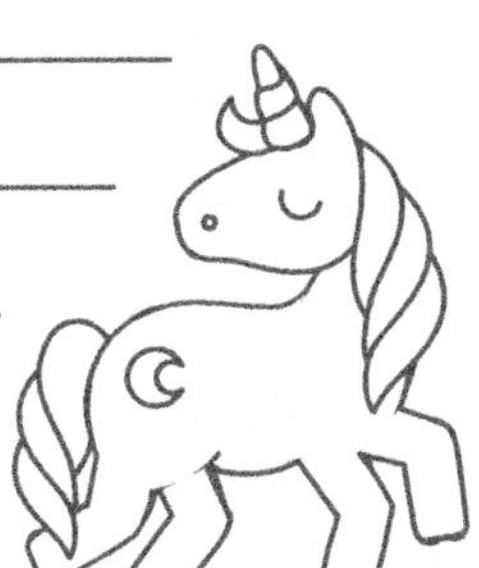

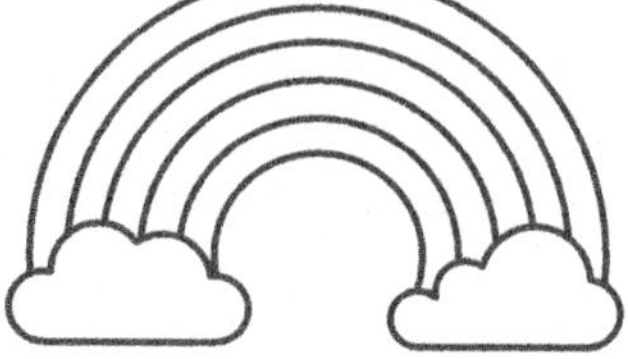

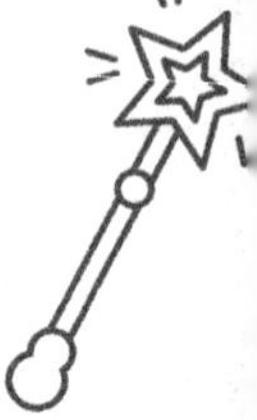

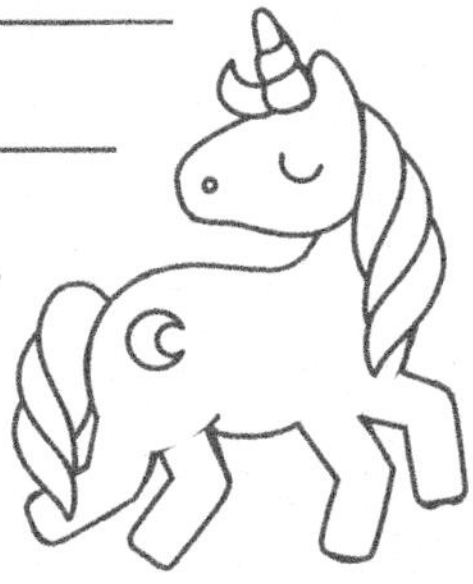

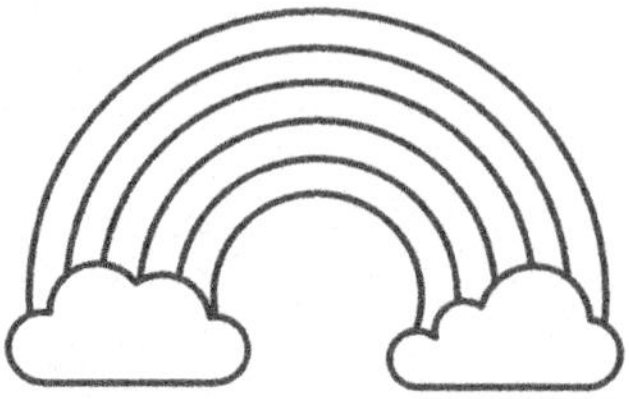

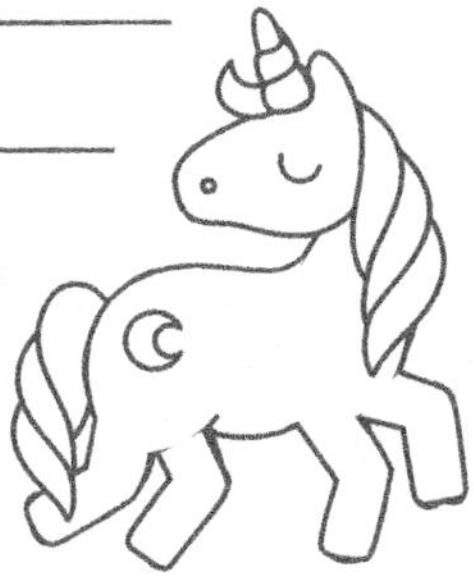

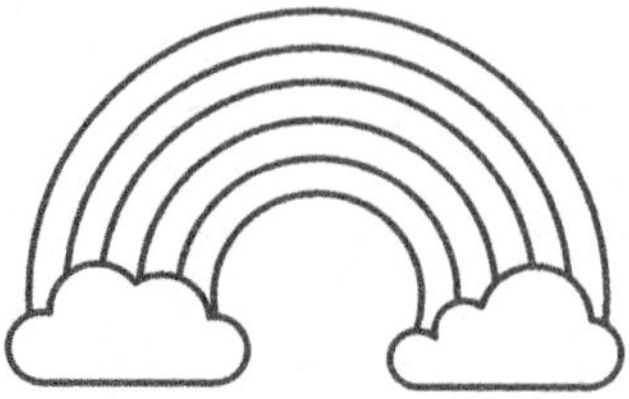
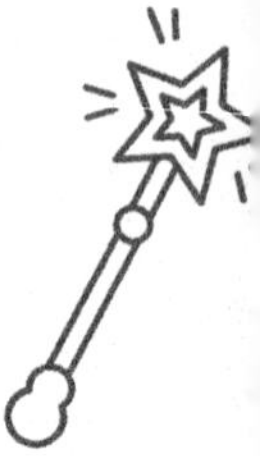

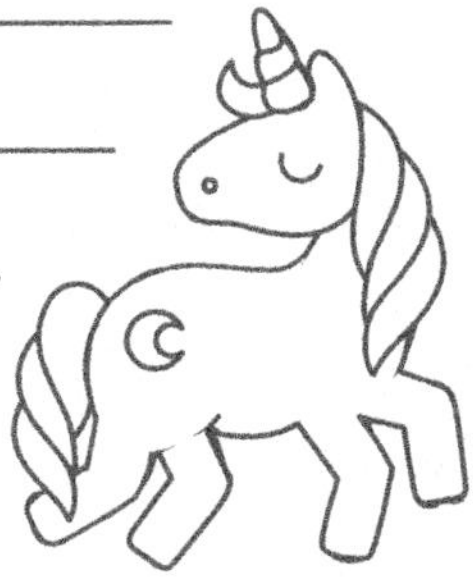

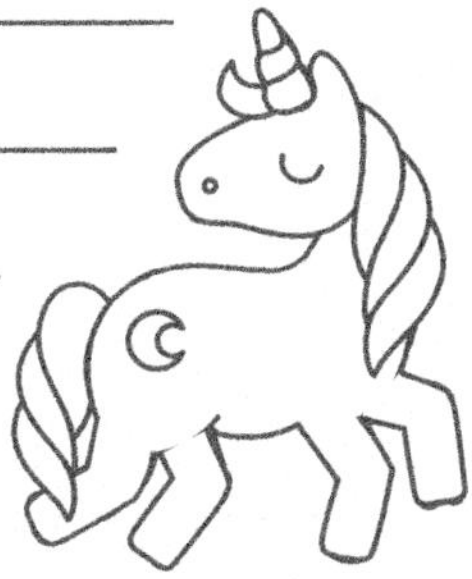

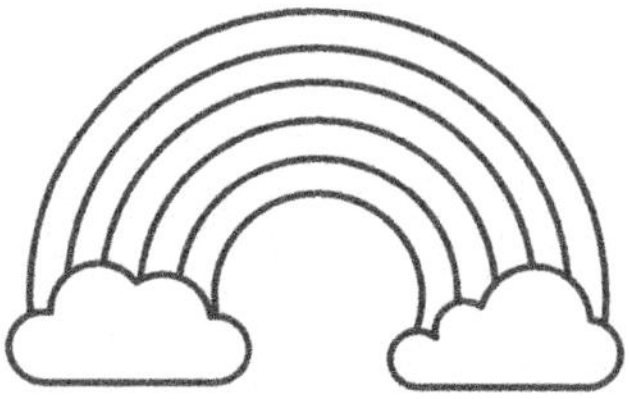

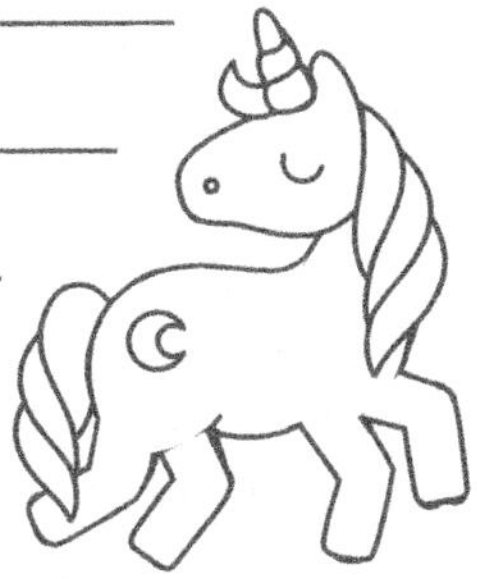

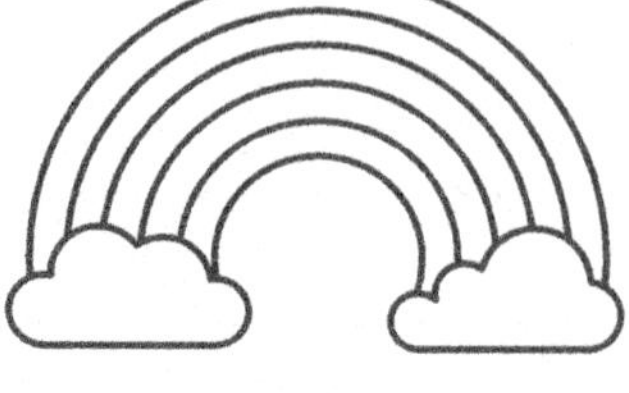
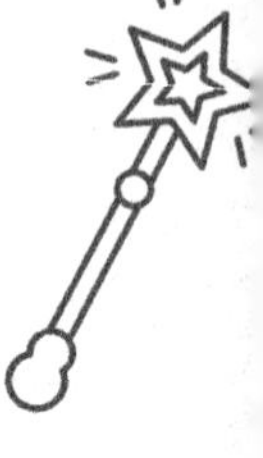

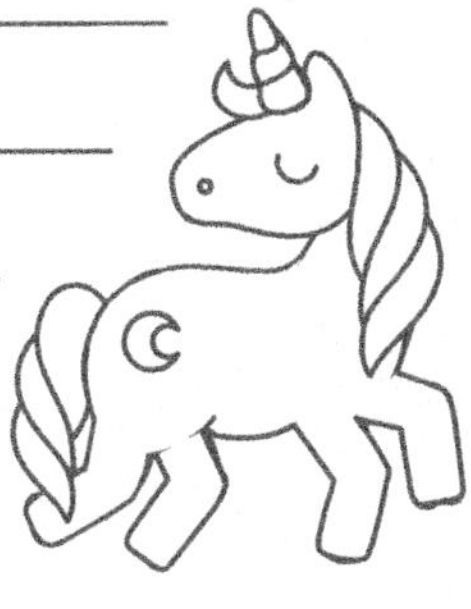

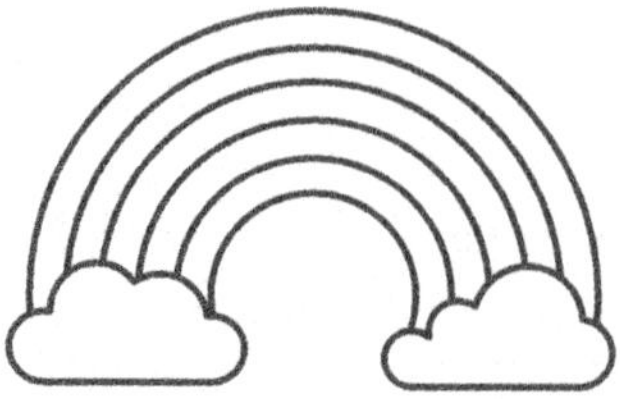
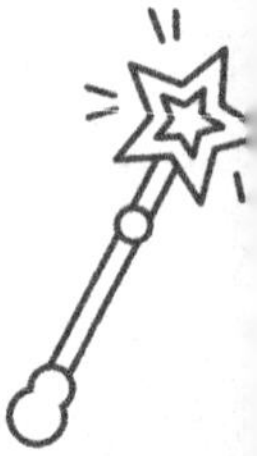

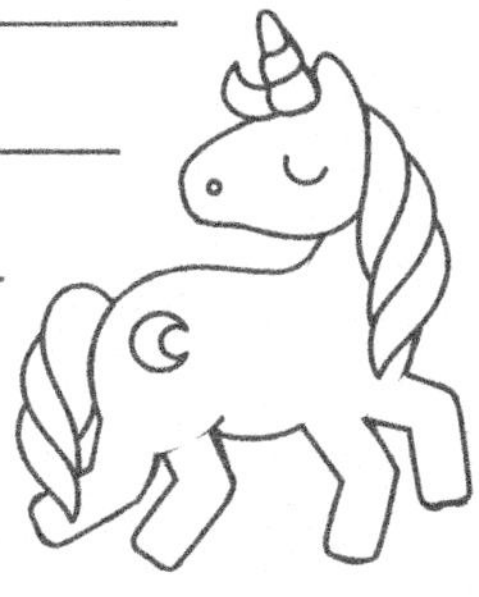

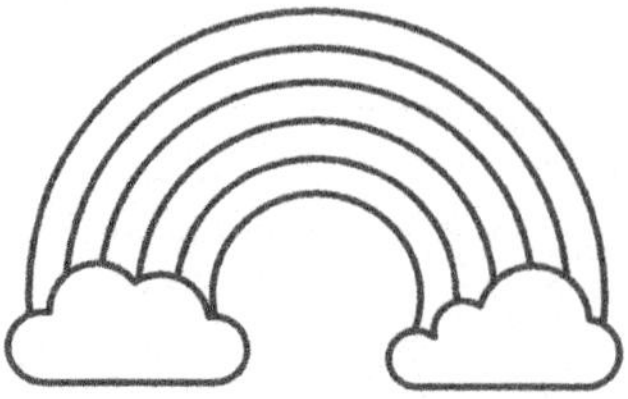

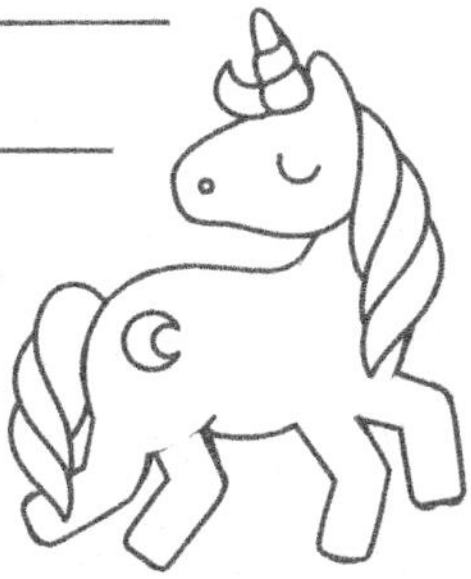

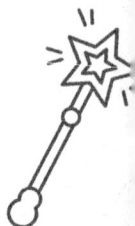

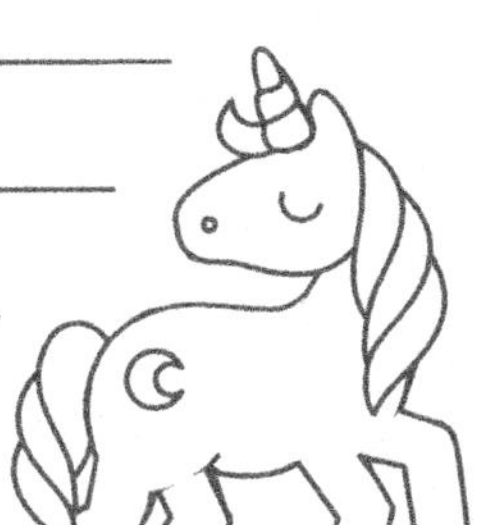

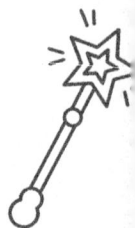

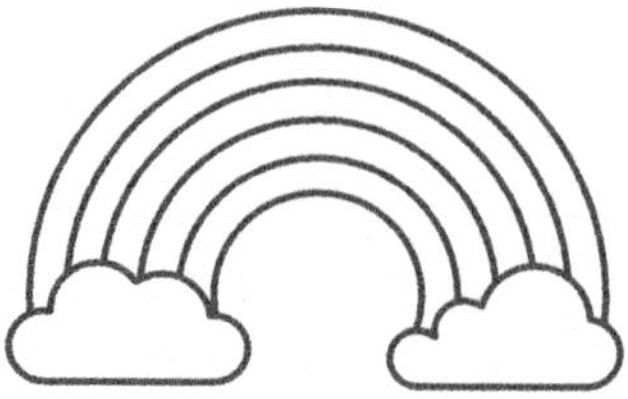

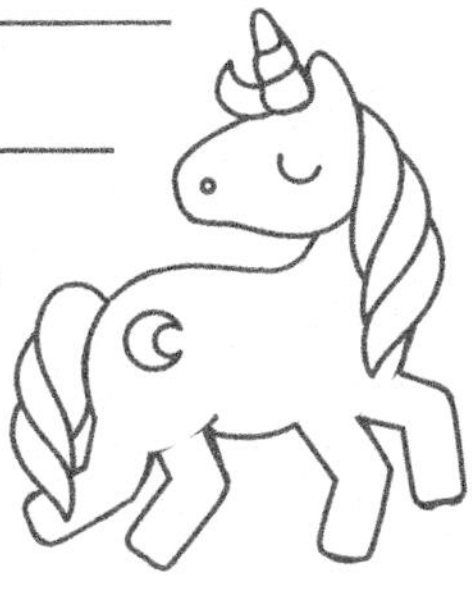

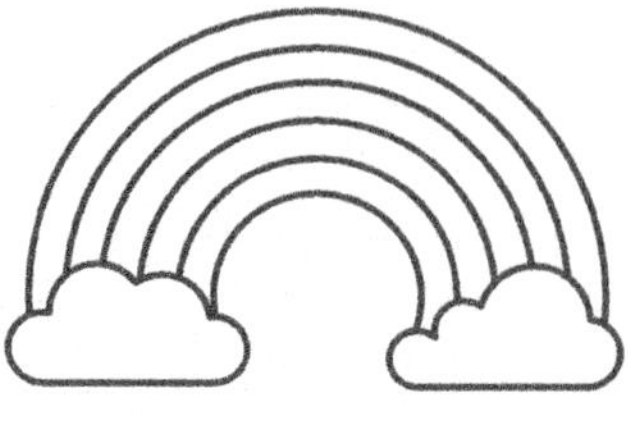

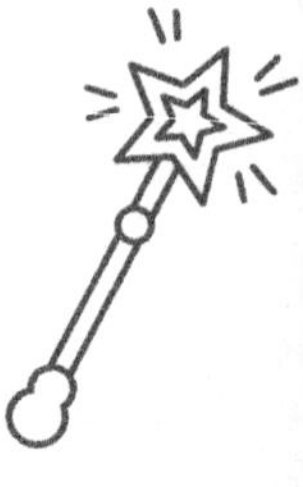

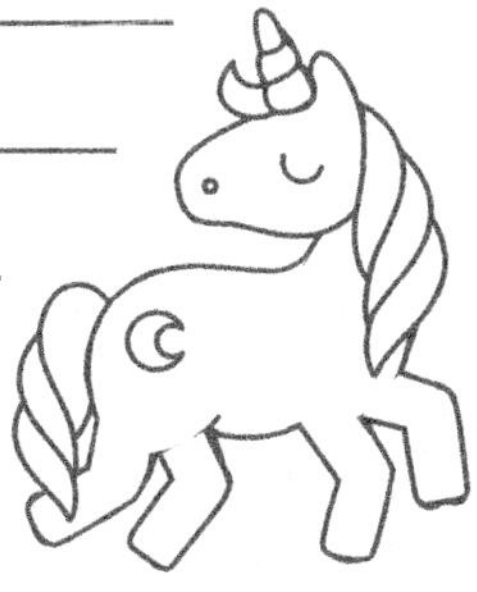

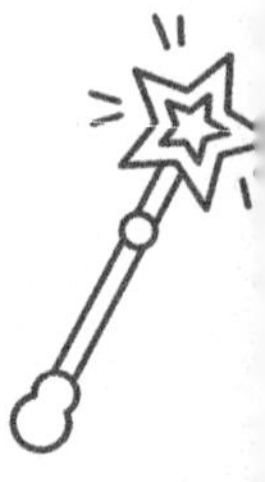
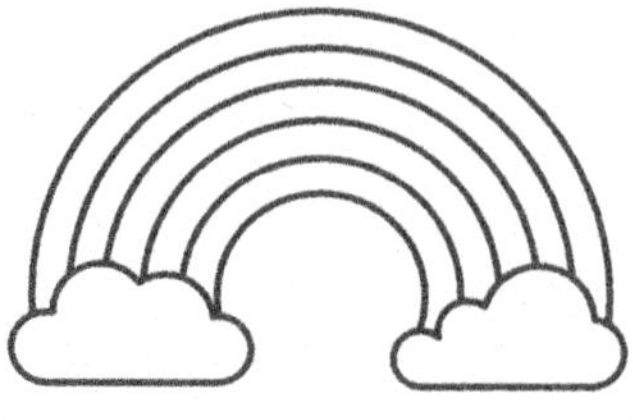

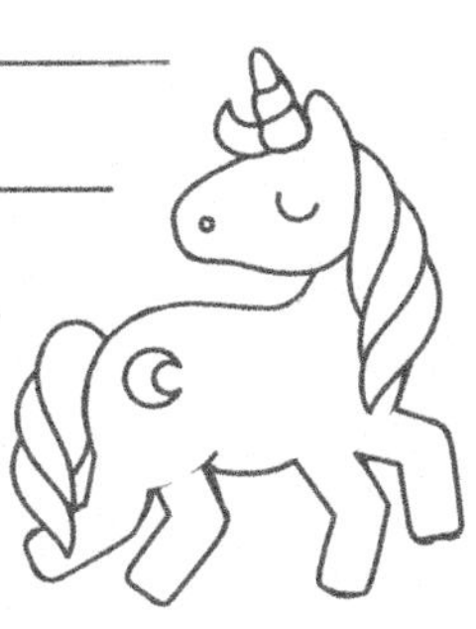

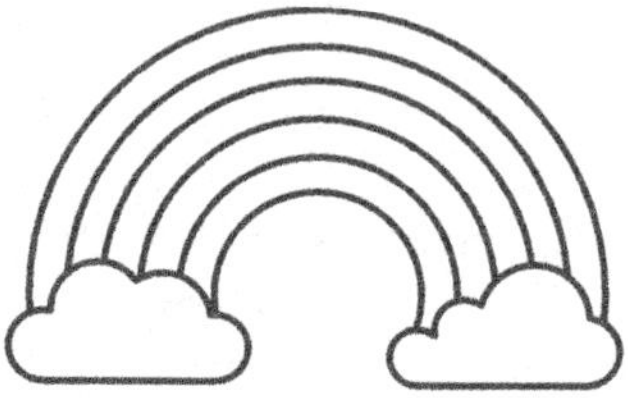
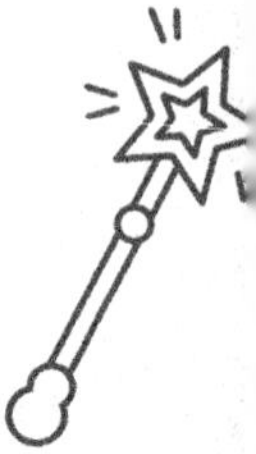

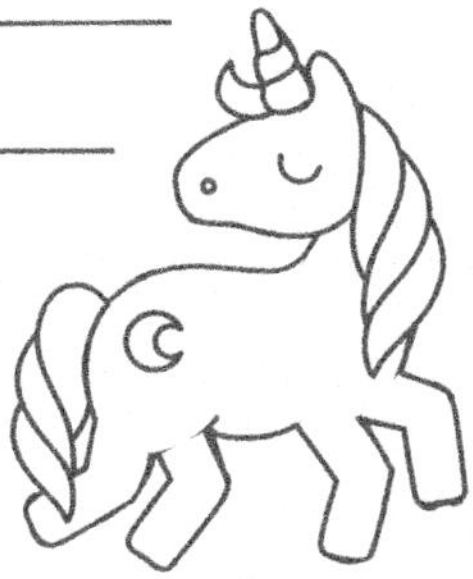

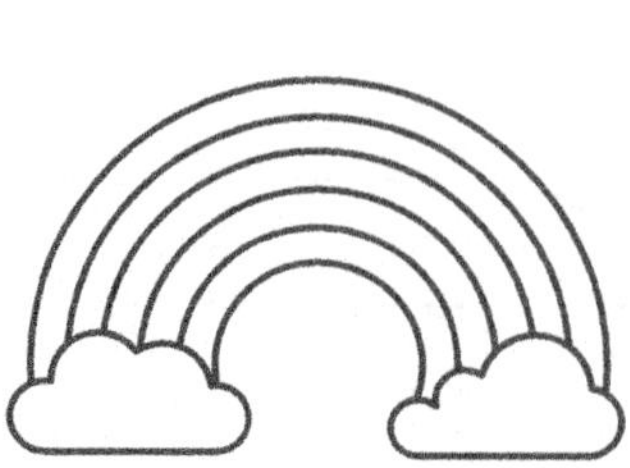

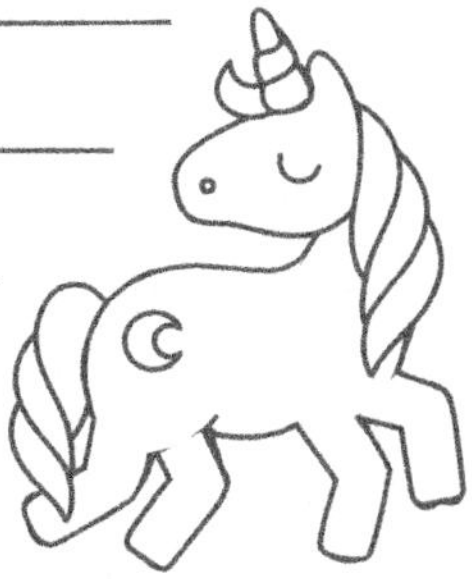

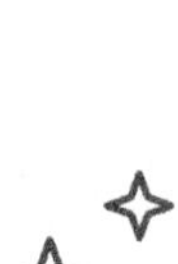
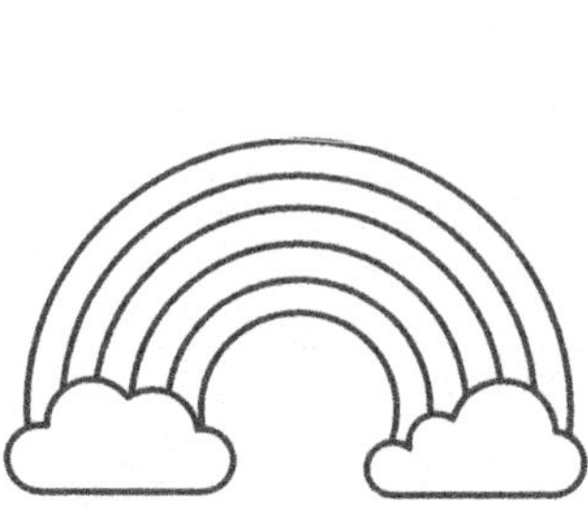
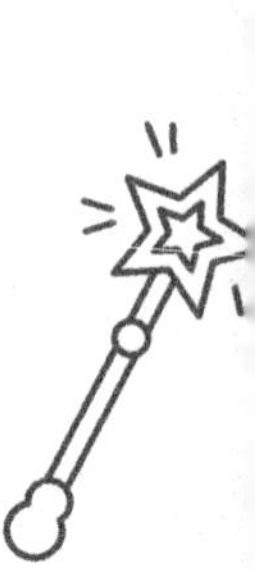

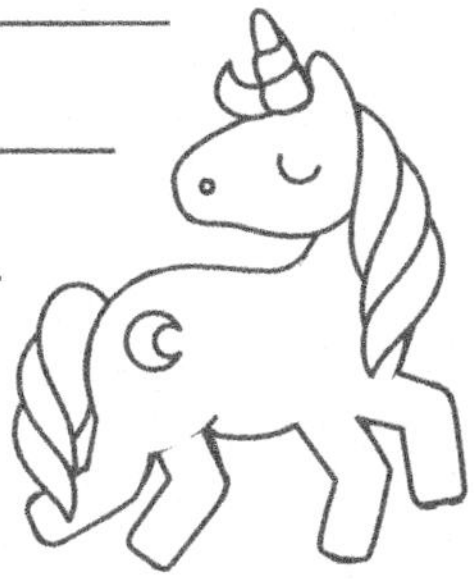

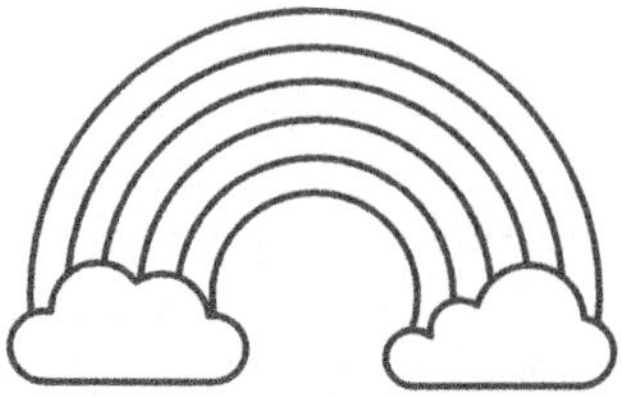

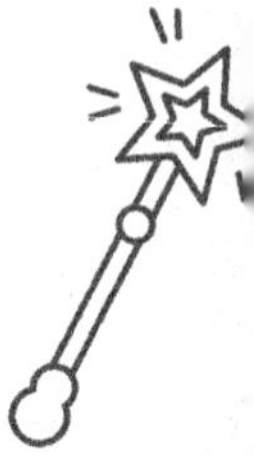

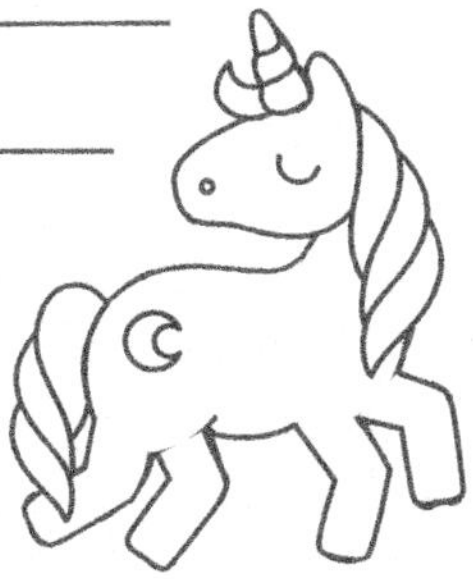

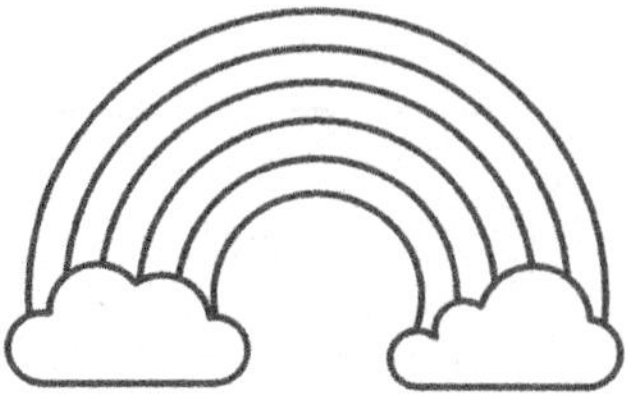

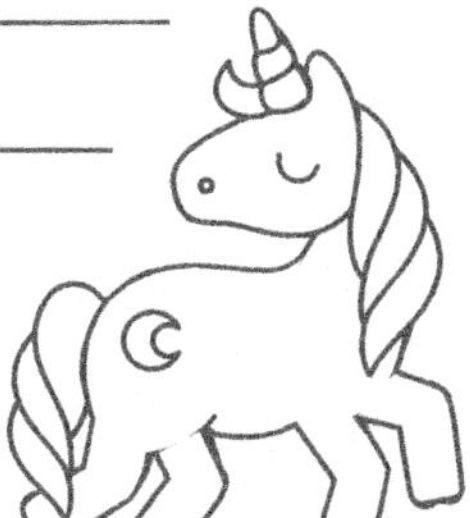

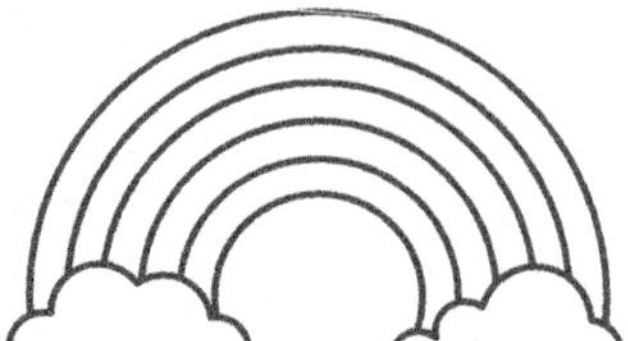

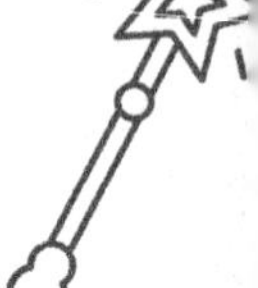

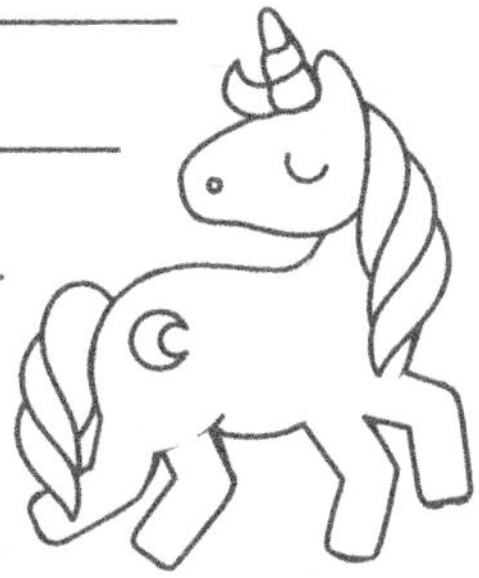

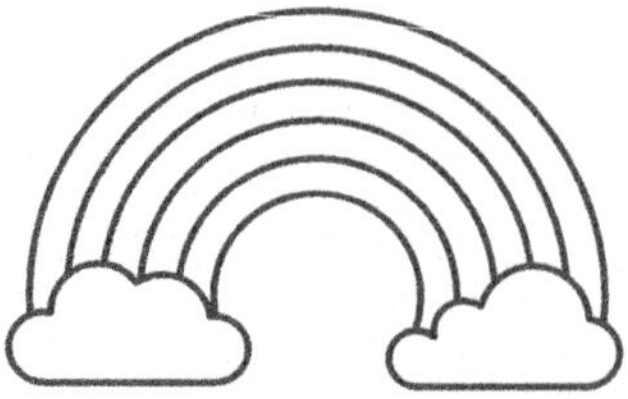

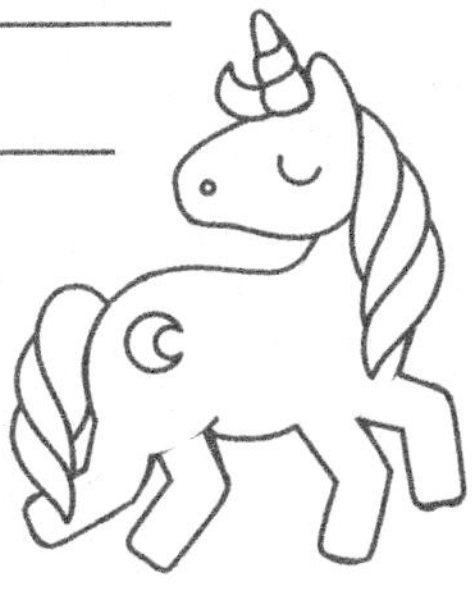

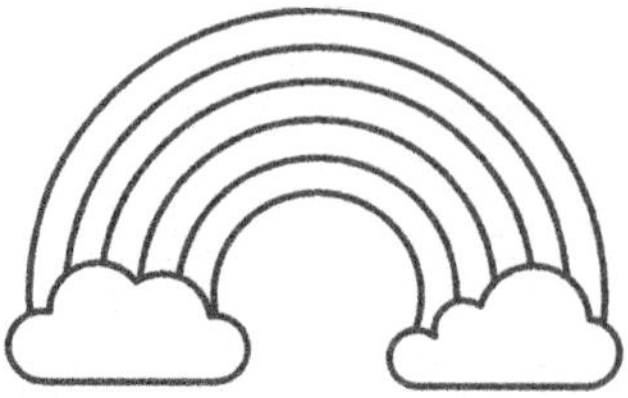

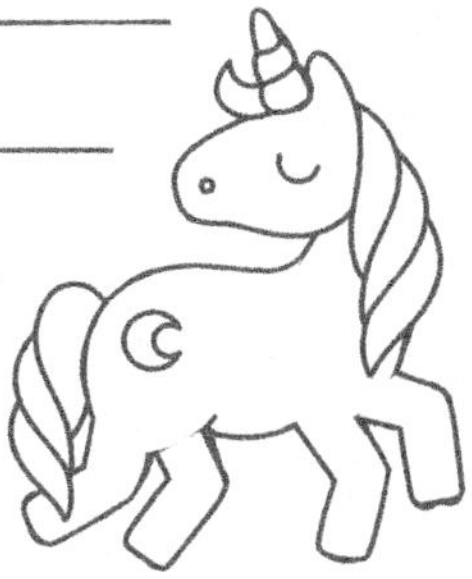

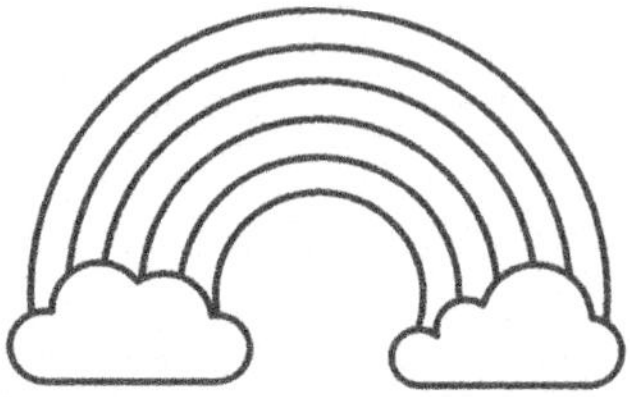
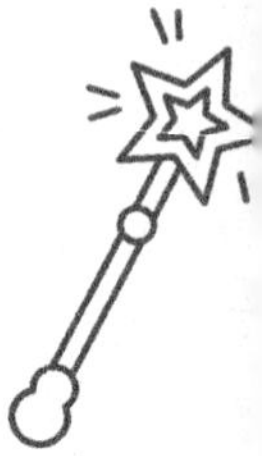

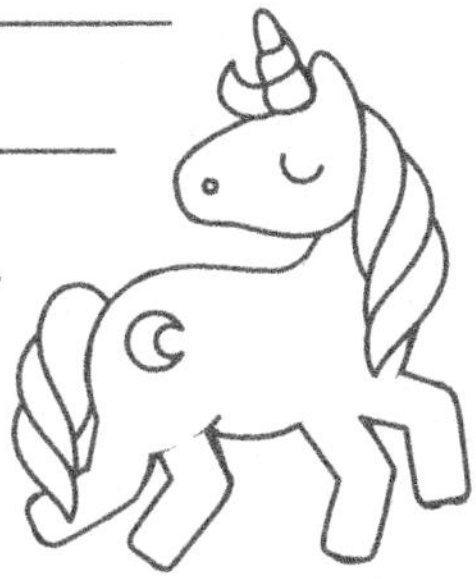

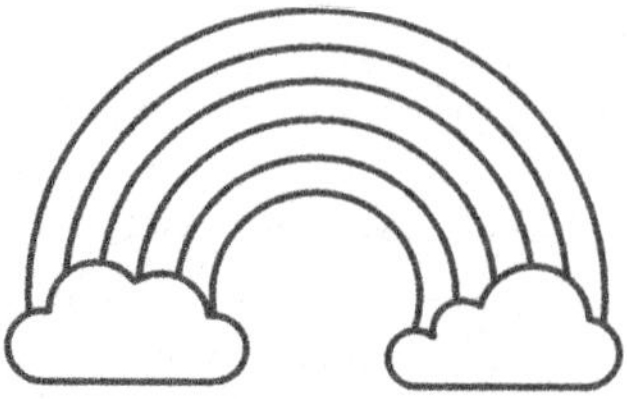
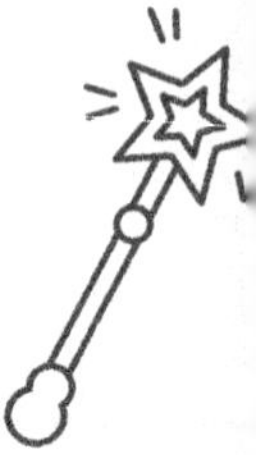

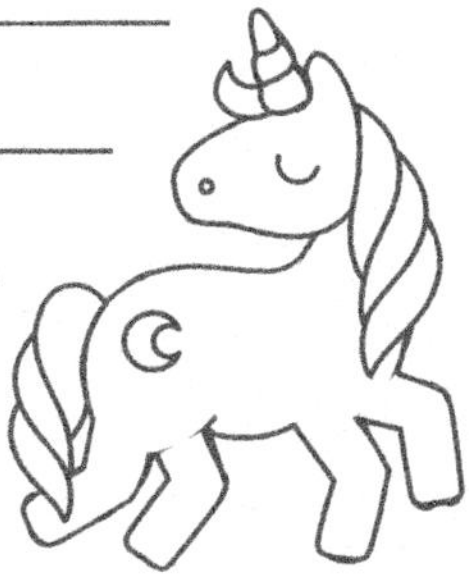

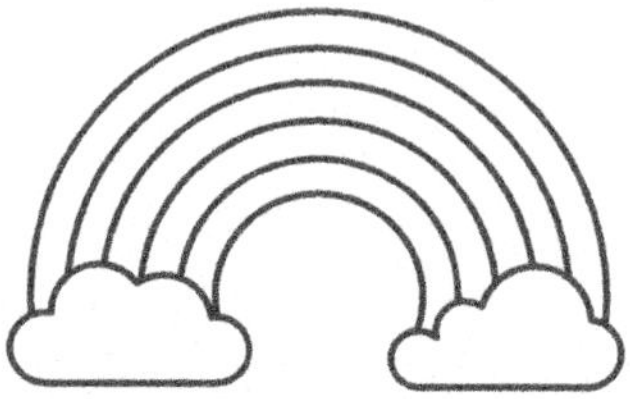

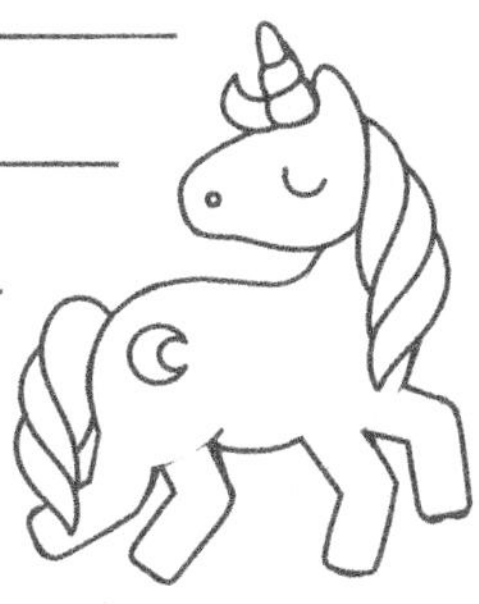

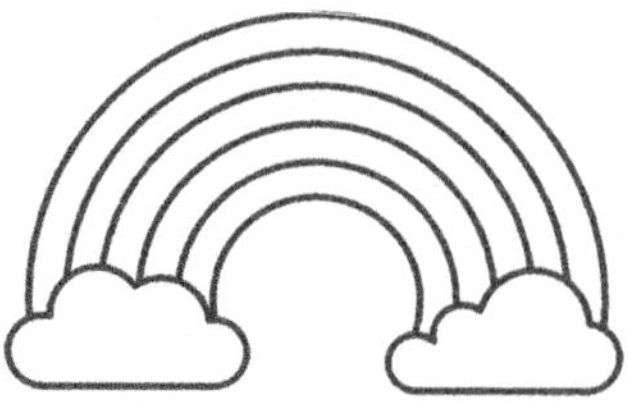

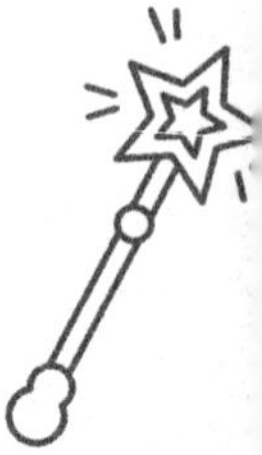

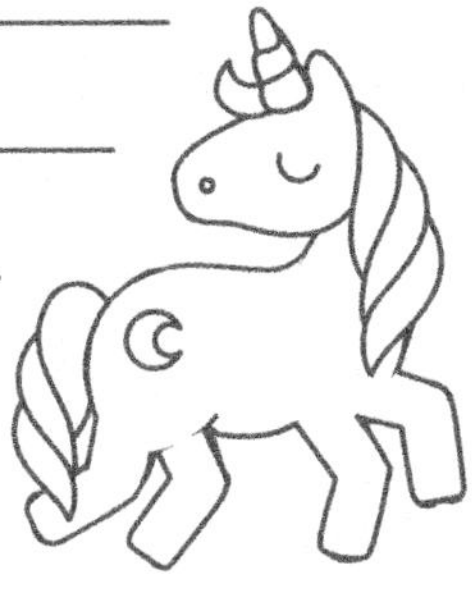

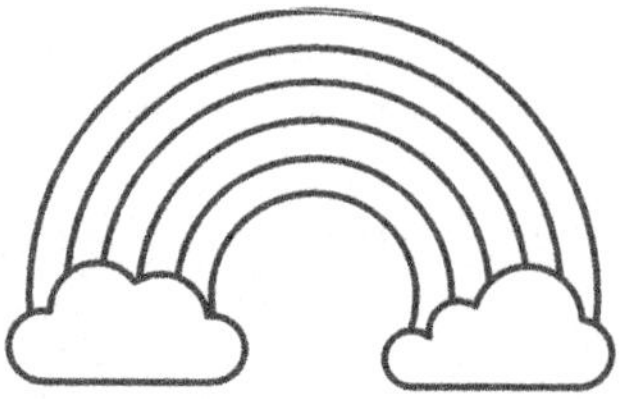

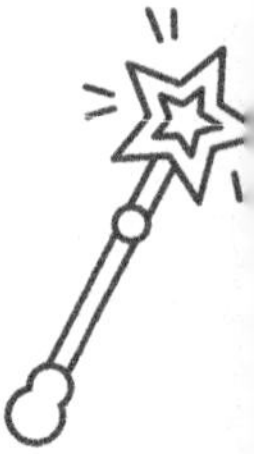

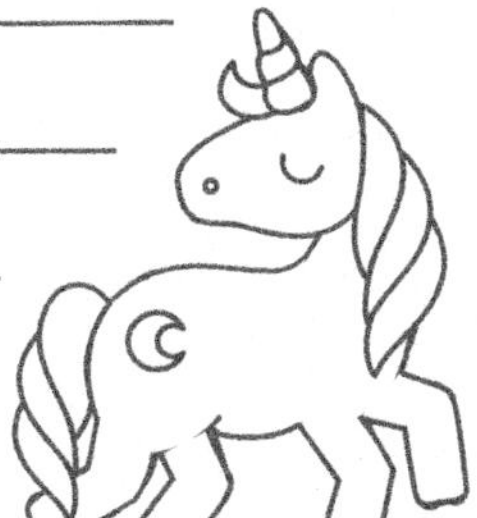

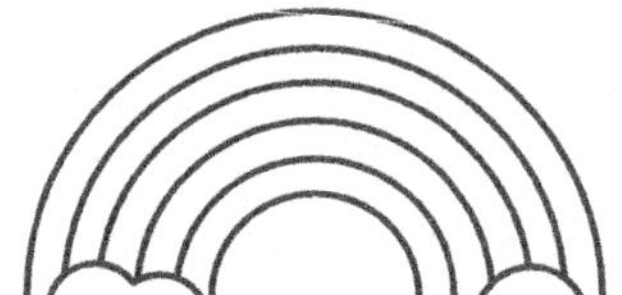

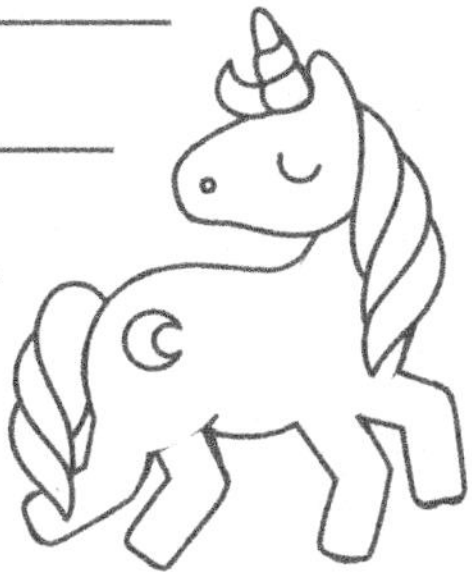

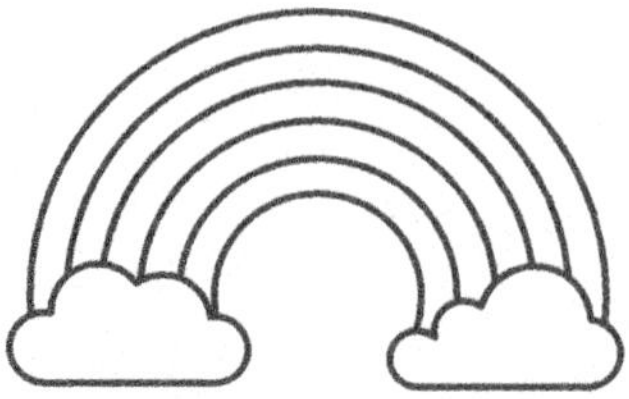

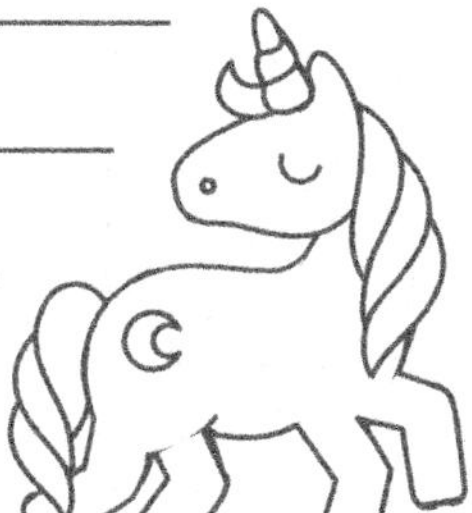

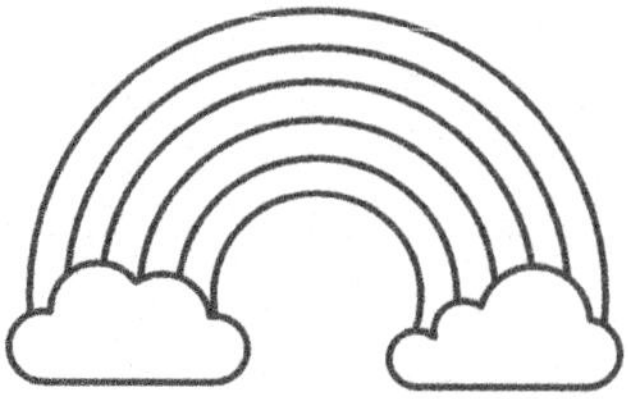

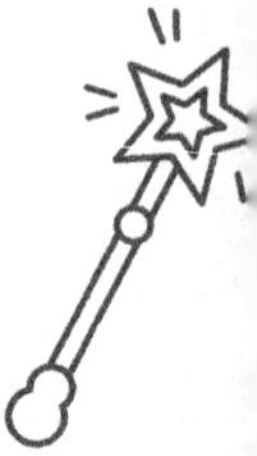

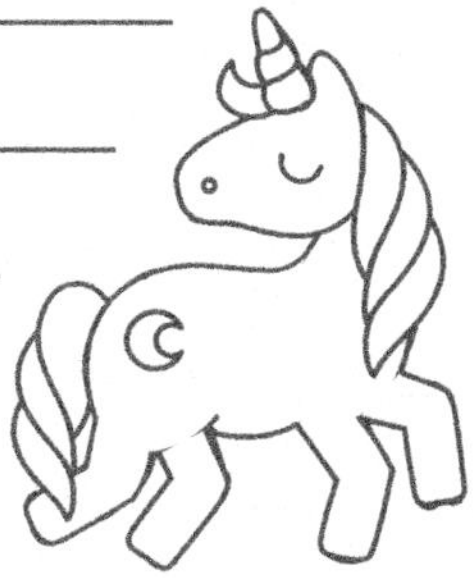

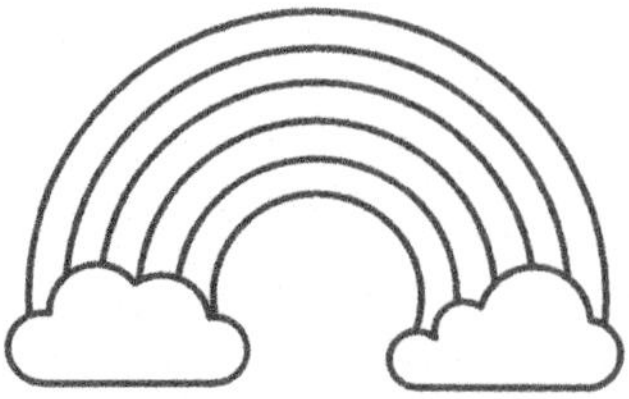

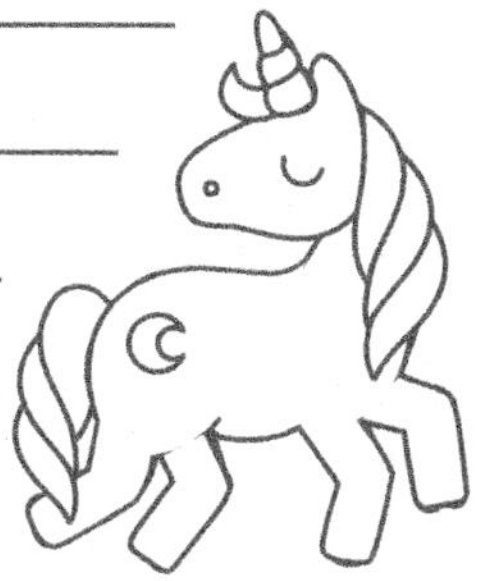

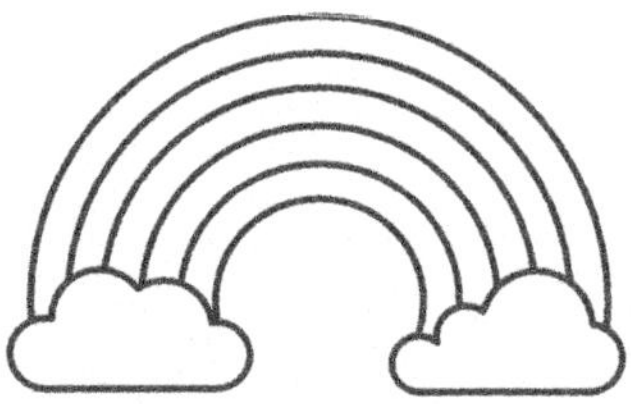
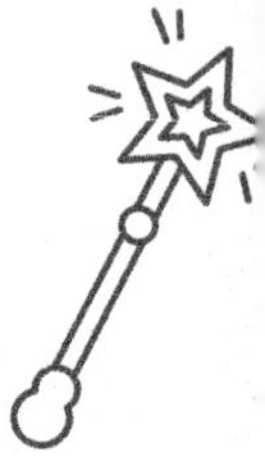

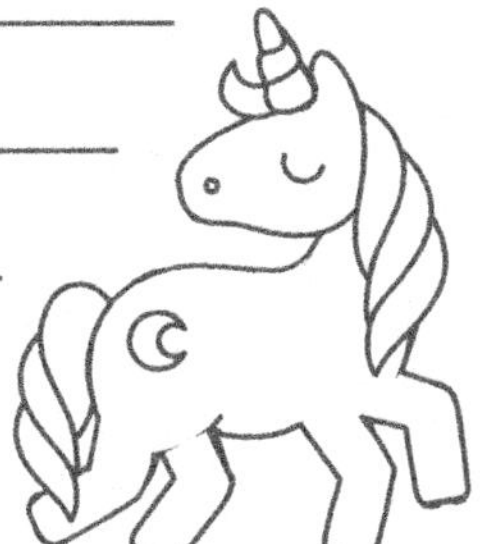

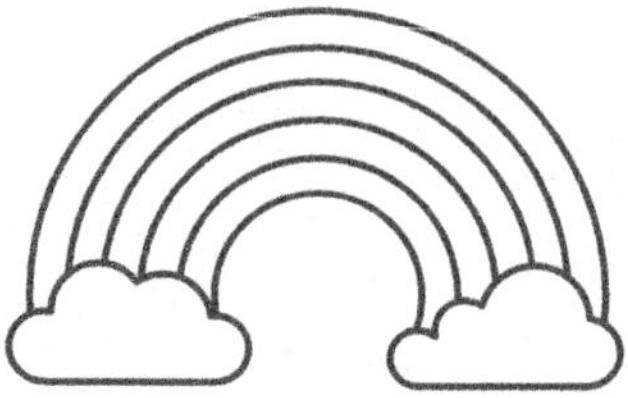

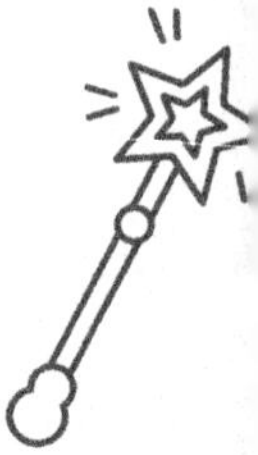

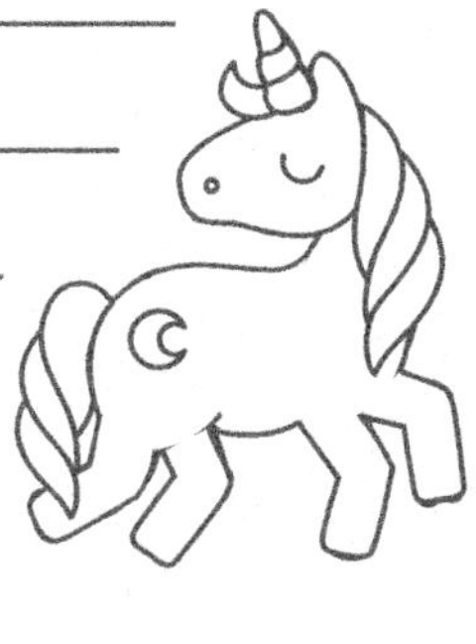

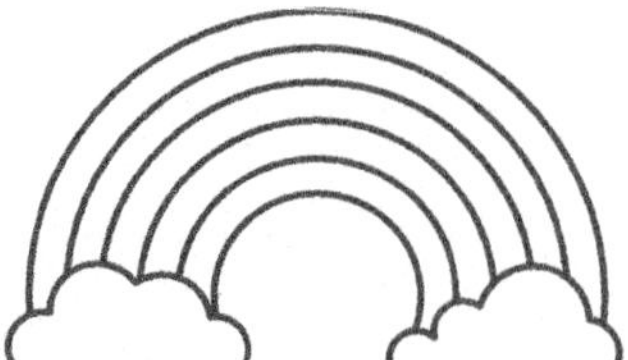

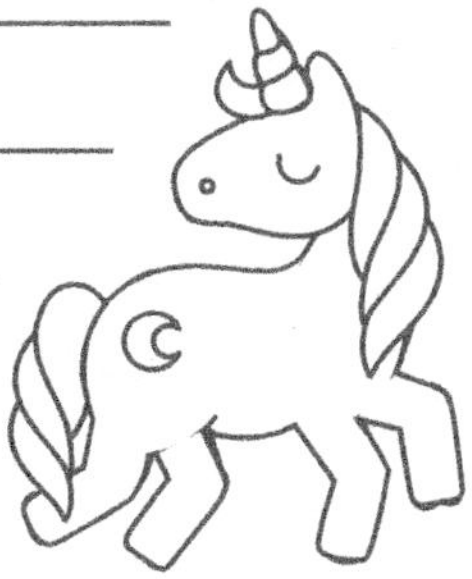

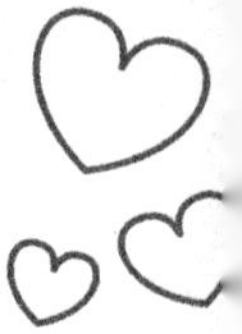

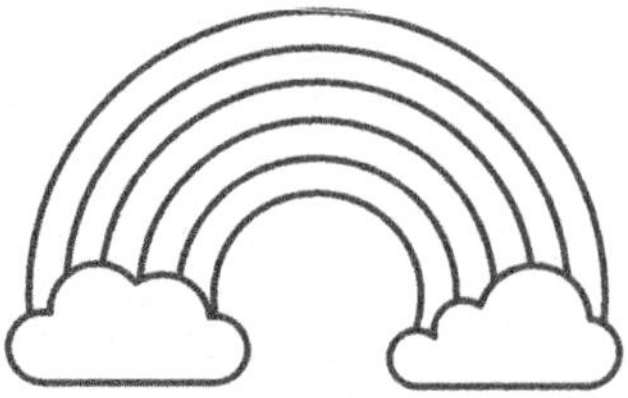

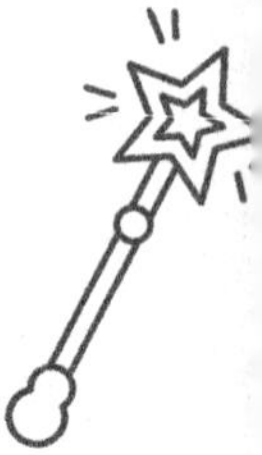

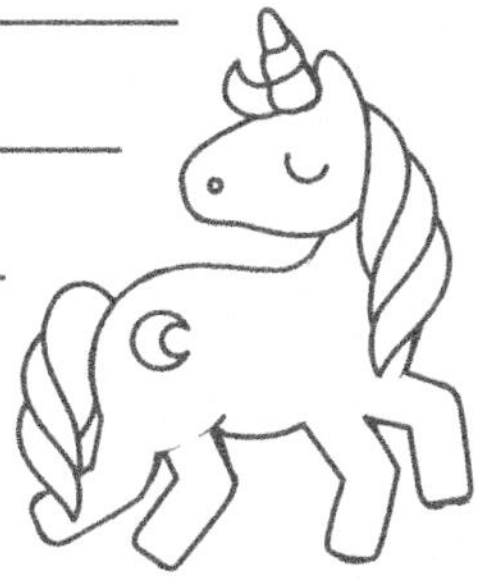

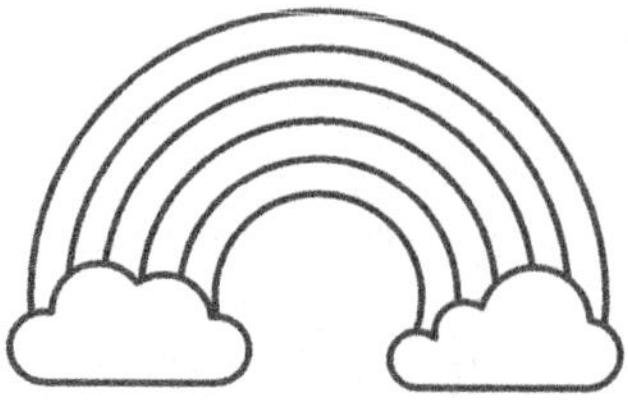
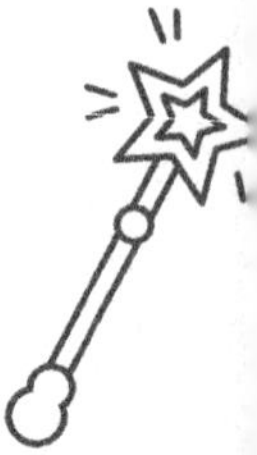

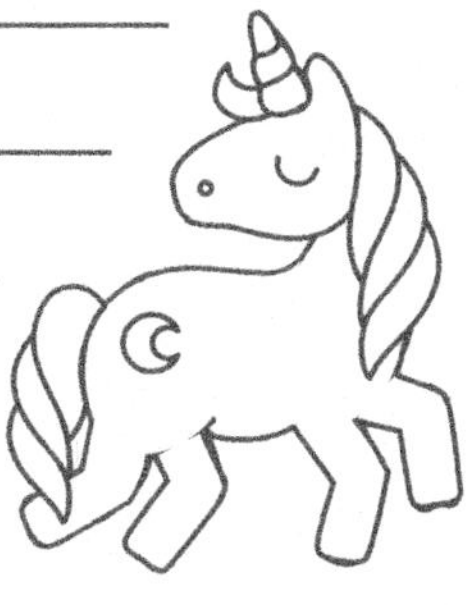

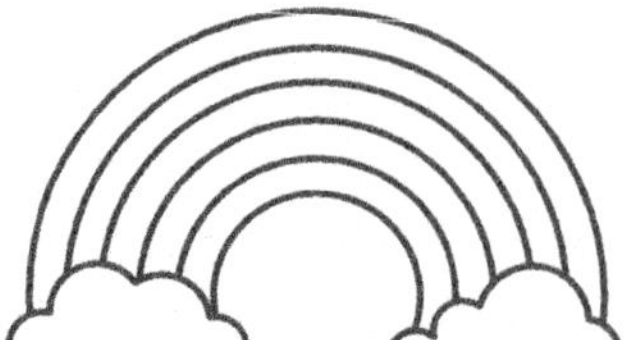

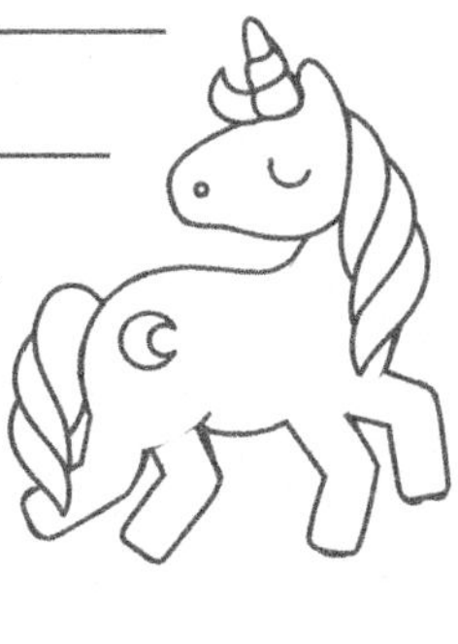

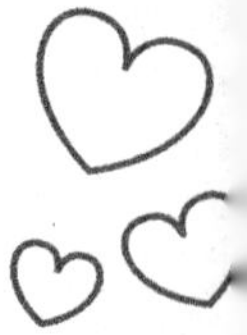

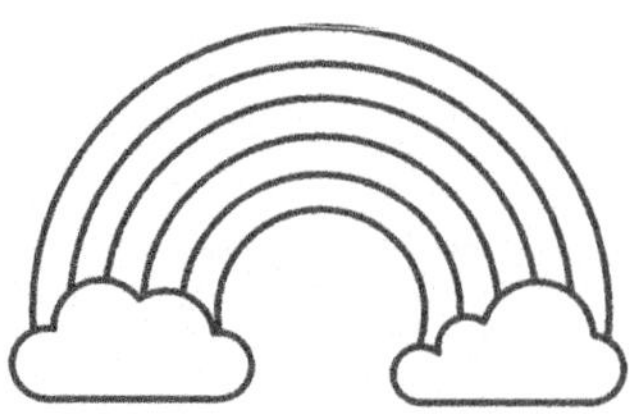

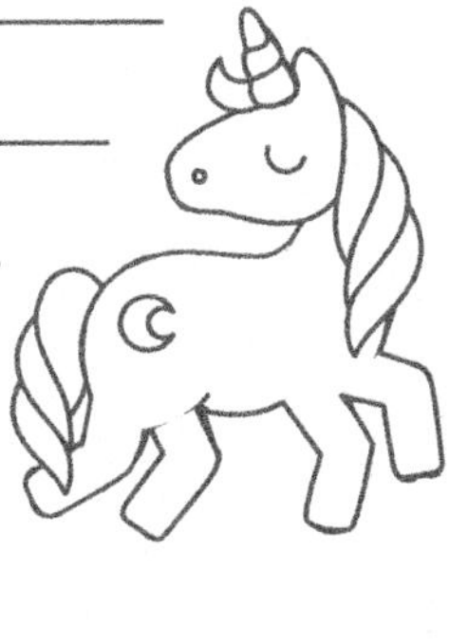

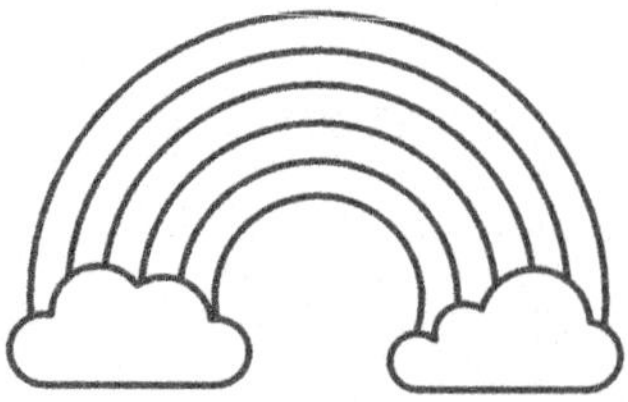

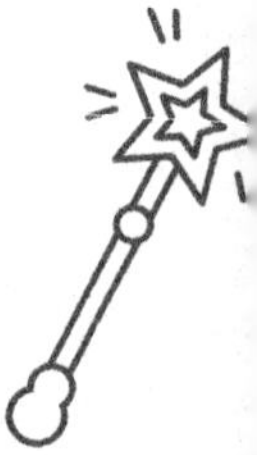

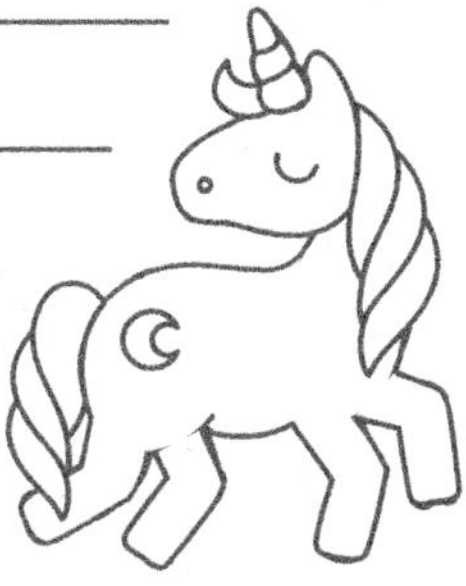

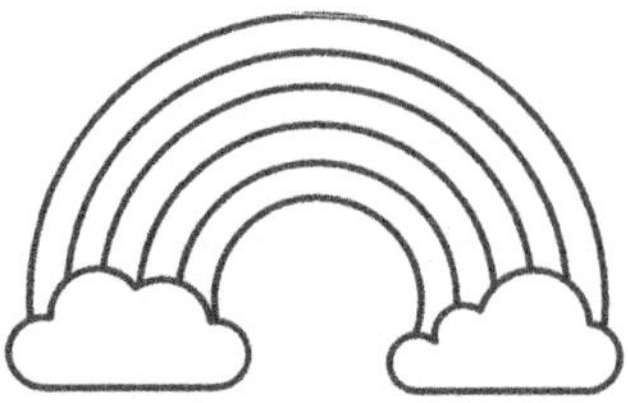

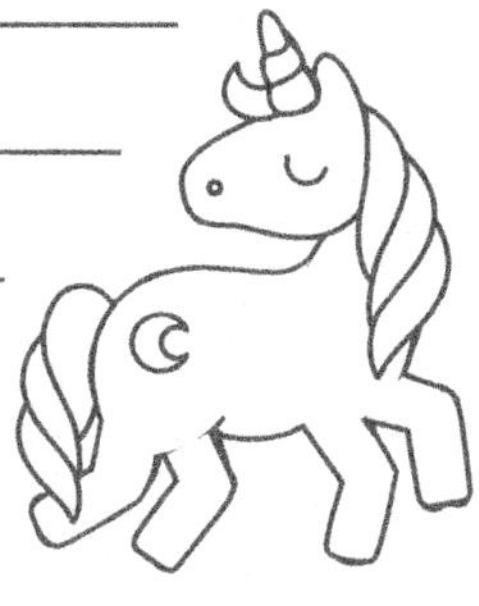

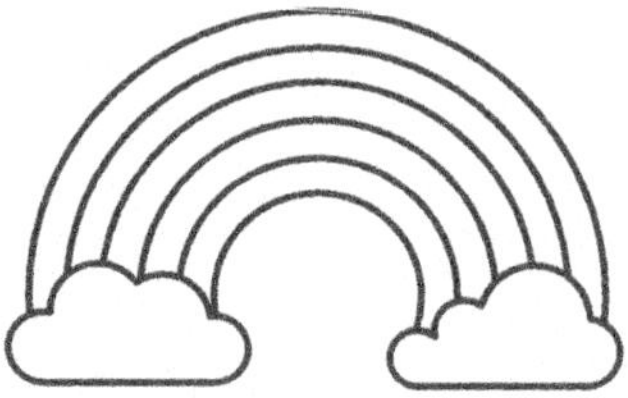

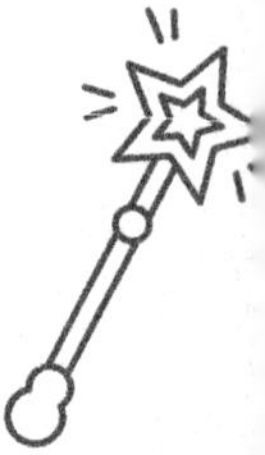

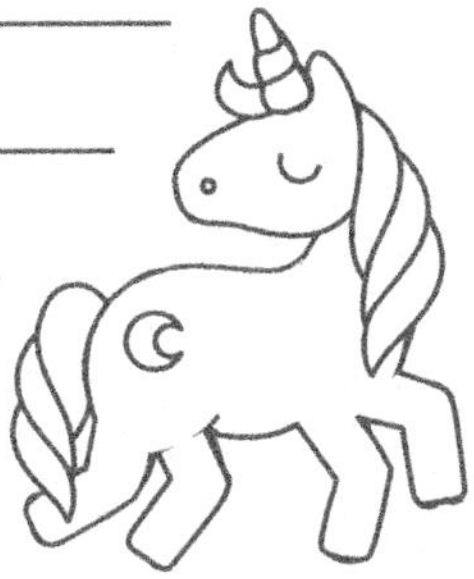

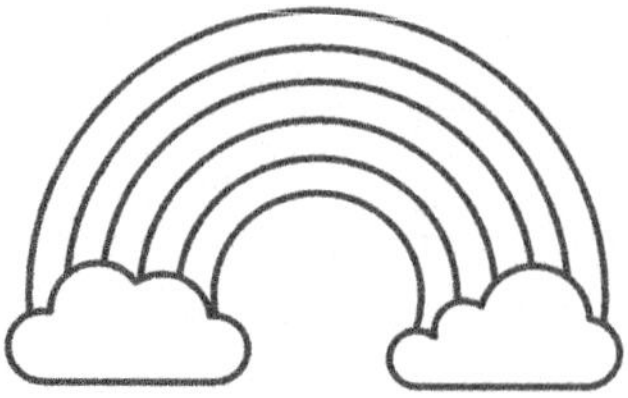
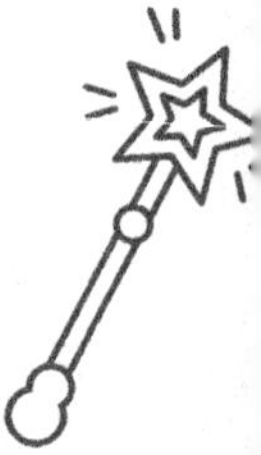

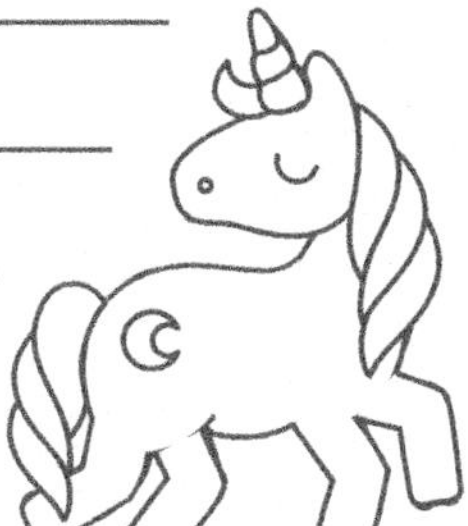

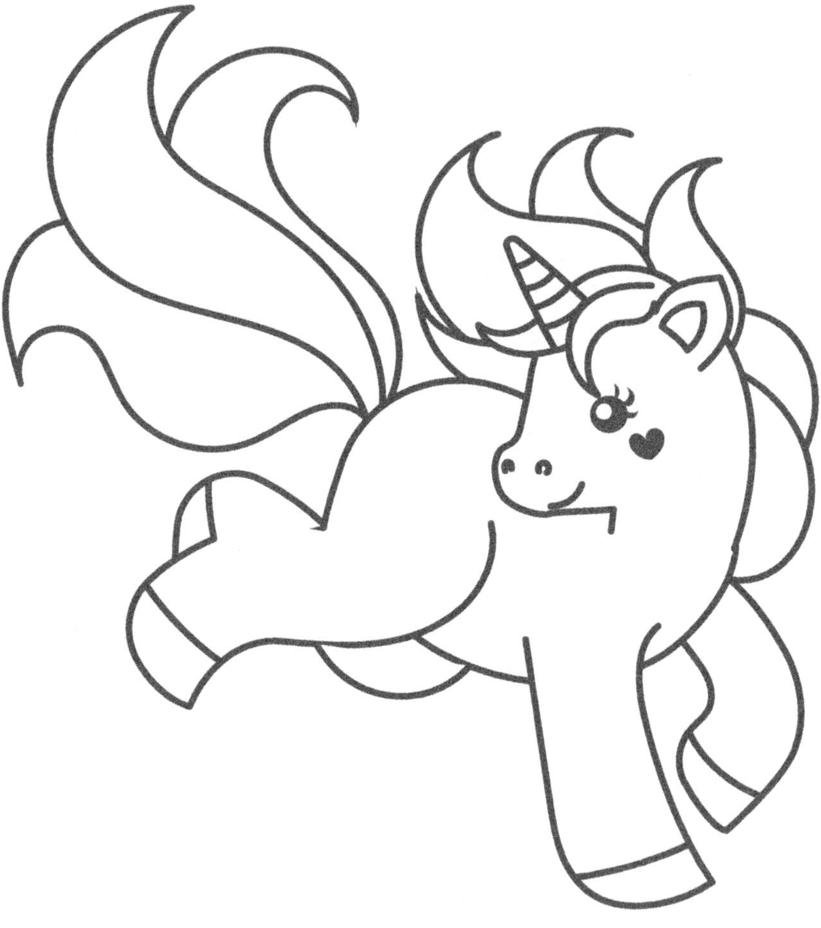

Made in the USA
Las Vegas, NV
10 December 2020

12498391R00056